LEADERS LIKE US
José Feliciano

BY ANNETTE M. CLAYTON

ILLUSTRATED BY ELISA CHAVARRI

Rourke.

Before Reading: *Building Background Knowledge and Vocabulary*

Building background knowledge can help children process new information and build upon what they already know. Before reading a book, it is important to tap into what children already know about the topic. This will help them develop their vocabulary and increase their reading comprehension.

Questions and Activities to Build Background Knowledge:

1. Look at the front cover of the book and read the title. What do you think this book will be about?
2. What do you already know about this topic?
3. Take a book walk and skim the pages. Look at the table of contents, photographs, captions, and bold words. Did these text features give you any information or predictions about what you will read in this book?

Vocabulary: *Vocabulary Is Key to Reading Comprehension*

Use the following directions to prompt a conversation about each word.

- Read the vocabulary words.
- What comes to mind when you see each word?
- What do you think each word means?

Vocabulary Words:
- blind
- cuatro
- immigrated
- impaired
- jazz
- nominated
- obstacle
- producer

During Reading: *Reading for Meaning and Understanding*

To achieve deep comprehension of a book, children are encouraged to use close reading strategies. During reading, it is important to have children stop and make connections. These connections result in deeper analysis and understanding of a book.

 Close Reading a Text

During reading, have children stop and talk about the following:

- Any confusing parts
- Any unknown words
- Text to text, text to self, text to world connections
- The main idea in each chapter or heading

Encourage children to use context clues to determine the meaning of any unknown words. These strategies will help children learn to analyze the text more thoroughly as they read.

When you are finished reading this book, turn to the next-to-last page for **Text-Dependent Questions** and an **Extension Activity**.

TABLE OF CONTENTS

MUSICAL DREAMS

Have you ever faced an **obstacle** on your way to achieving a goal? Have you ever felt like it was too hard to overcome?

José Feliciano knows what it's like to overcome challenges. He was born **blind** and didn't grow up with money. Still, José wanted to be a musician. He taught himself to play the guitar. His music united people of different backgrounds.

José sat nervously in the audience. It was the 1968 Grammys, an important music award ceremony. José was **nominated** for Best New Artist. He was only 23 years old. José never imagined his music would be so popular.

And the winner is...

José Feliciano!

Fans cheered. José took a deep breath. It was a dream come true.

10-FINGERED WIZARD

José Feliciano was born in Lares, Puerto Rico, in 1945. He was born blind and his family had little money. But what they had plenty of was a love of music. José's uncle had a **cuatro**. Three-year-old José would play music with him.

José's family eventually **immigrated** to New York City. When José was nine, a family friend noticed his interest in music. He bought José a guitar. José fell in love with the instrument. He taught himself to play by listening to records—sometimes practicing 14 hours a day.

BLIND FROM BIRTH

José was born with congenital glaucoma. It made him blind. It is a rare eye condition.

José grew up in Harlem, listening to **jazz** and rock and roll. The tunes moved him. He began to sing along.

By the age of seventeen, José quit school to earn money. He played his music at coffee houses. Tips tumbled into his hat. A music **producer** from RCA Records saw José playing at a club in Greenwich Village. He signed José to their label.

A CULTURAL HOT SPOT
Greenwich Village is in Manhattan, New York City. It is popular location for musicians, artist, and politicians. Famous musicians, such as Jimi Hendrix, were discovered there.

In 1964, José released his first single "Everybody Do the Click." Soon, he released his first folk-pop-soul album, *The Voice and Guitar of José Feliciano*. He quickly followed it with the album *A Bag Full of Soul*. He was so talented on the guitar that reviewers nicknamed him the "10-Fingered Wizard."

After many successful tours and more albums, José became a household name in Latin America.

INTO THE SPOTLIGHT

José was invited to sing the national anthem at a baseball game in 1968. He loved his country and came up with his own take on the Star-Spangled Banner.

**His version was slow and soulful...
...a mix of Latin and jazz music...
...José poured his love of
America into the song.**

Some fans booed. They didn't like that he strayed from the original tune. José was devasted. But many fans loved it. José's version become popular. It reached the top 50 music charts. José's version led to many other artists creating their own versions of the national anthem.

José was a trailblazer in more than just music. He was an advocate for people like him, who used guide dogs to get around. The dogs were not welcomed in some theaters. José didn't think this was right and he wanted to do something about it. He wrote a song called "No Dogs Allowed." José likes to think his song helped make changes to the law.

ANIMAL HELPERS

Guide dogs are trained to guide people who are blind or visually **impaired** around objects. The most common breeds trained as guide dogs are German shepherds, labrador retrievers, and golden retrievers.

In 1970, José wrote "Feliz Navidad." It is a Christmas song in both English and Spanish. He hoped it would unite people with Christmas cheer.

José was right. People couldn't get enough of the song. It played over and over again on the radio. It remains one of the most popular Christmas songs in the world.

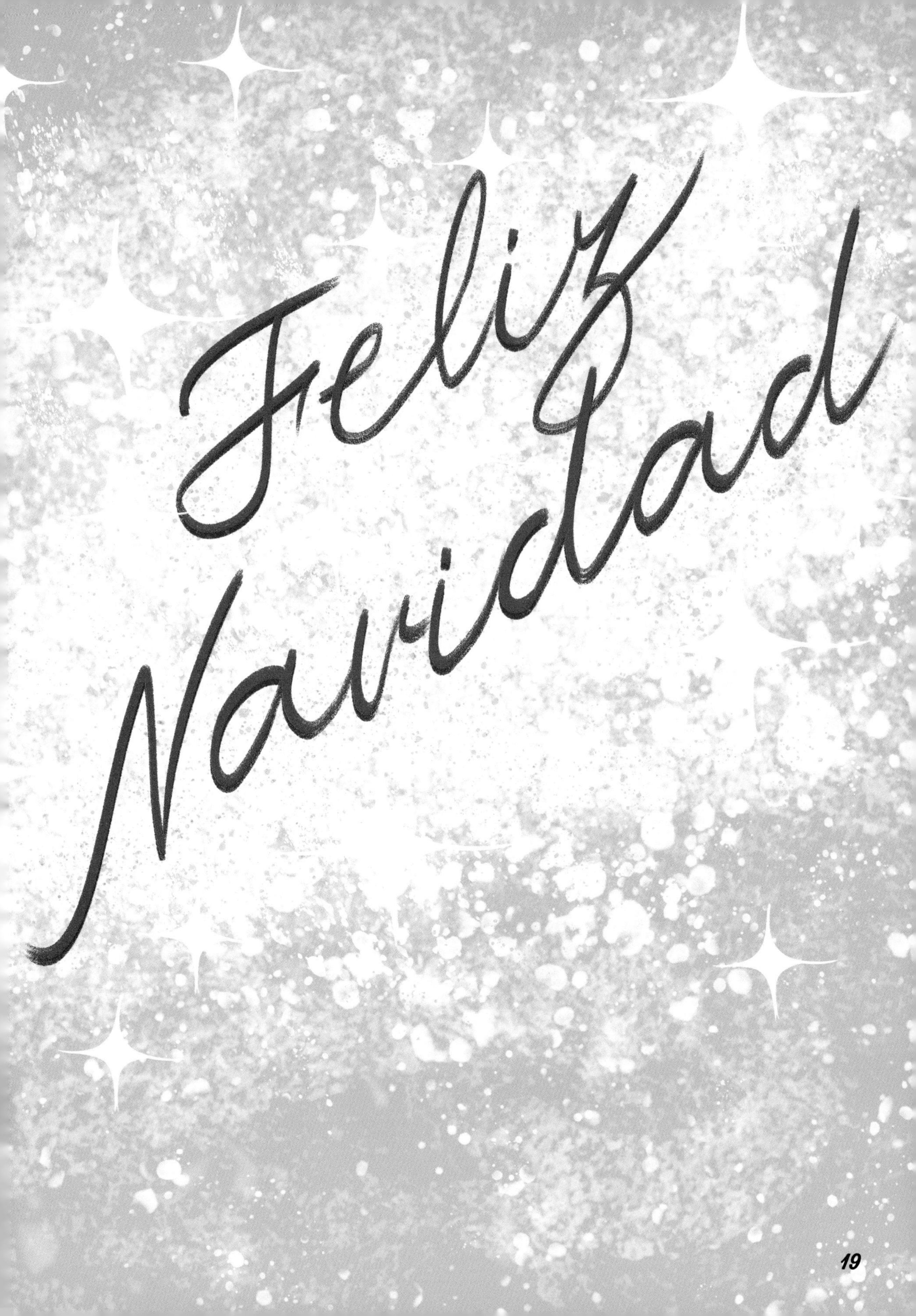
Feliz
Navidad

José has had an amazing career. By 2022, he had received nine Grammy awards and 45 gold and platinum records.

Throughout his career, José spread his message of unity through his music. His songs have brought together people of different races, backgrounds, and beliefs. José wants to let young people with disabilities know that anything is possible.

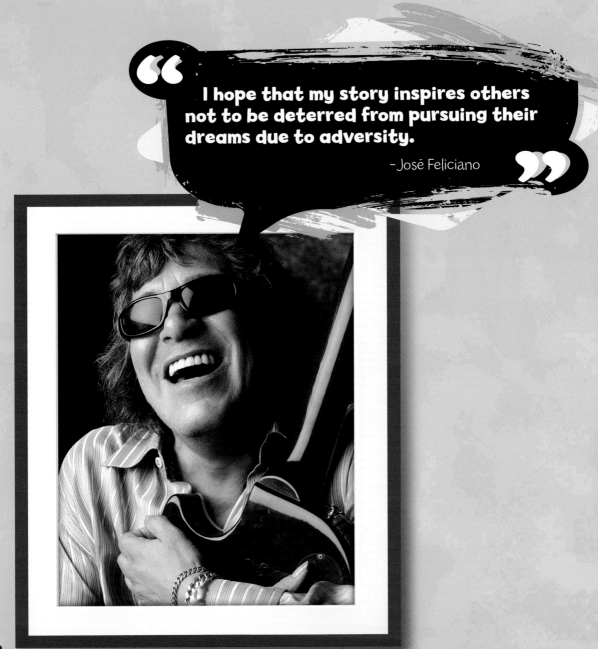

" I hope that my story inspires others not to be deterred from pursuing their dreams due to adversity.

–José Feliciano

TIME LINE

1945   José was born on September 10, in Lares, Puerto Rico.

1948   José's love of music begins when he plays a tin cracker can with his uncle.

1963   José is signed to RCA's record label.

1964   José's first single, "Everybody Do The Click," is released.

1967   While playing music in England, José's guide dog was not allowed in theaters.

1968   José wins Best New Artist at the Grammys.

1968   José sings a soulful version of the National Anthem. It receives mixed reviews.

1969   José releases the song "No Dogs Allowed."

1970   José writes "Feliz Navidad," one of the most popular Christmas songs in the world.

1996   José receives Billboard's Lifetime Achievement Award.

GLOSSARY

blind (blinde): not able to see

cuatro (KWAH-tro): a small guitar with four or five strings, very popular in Puerto Rico

immigrated (im-i-GRAY-ted): to have come to live permanently in a foreign country

impaired (im-PAIRED): something that has been damaged and made less effective

jazz (jaz): a type of music started by African Americans with strong rhythm that does not follow written notes

nominated (NAH-muh-nay-ted): to have suggested someone would be good for a job or should receive an honor

obstacle (AHB-stuh-kuhl): something that makes it difficult to achieve something

producer (pruh-DOOS-ur): a person who oversees or finances a work of some kind, such as an artist's music, for distribution to the public

INDEX

TEXT-DEPENDENT QUESTIONS

1. How did José learn to play the guitar?

2. What where some obstacles José faced?

3. How is José a leader in music?

4. What is the title of José's most famous Christmas song?

5. Why did José write the song "No Dogs Allowed?"

EXTENSION ACTIVITY

Everyone faces challenges. Some are physical, like being blind. Some are emotional, like being scared. A challenge can also be a situation, like parents getting a divorce. What is a challenge in your life? How can you keep moving forward and chasing your dreams? Write down your ideas, then put them into action.

ABOUT THE AUTHOR

Annette M. Clayton is an author living in Maryland with her twin daughters, husband, and one fluffy cat. Like José, she has Puerto Rican roots and hopes to share stories that will inspire children's imaginations, spark creativity, and foster inclusivity. One her favorite activities is hiking on the Appalachian Trail. When it's too cold for that, you can find her inside, drinking lattes and reading a good book.

ABOUT THE ILLUSTRATOR

Elisa Chavarri is an award-winning illustrator who strives to create work that inspires happiness, promotes inclusiveness and curiosity, and helps people of all different backgrounds feel special. She has illustrated numerous books for children including the Pura Belpré Honor book *Sharuko: El Arqueólogo Peruano/Peruvian Archaeologist Julio C. Tello*. Elisa hails from Lima, Peru, and resides in Alpena, Michigan, with her husband and two young children.

© 2024 Rourke Educational Media

www.rourkebooks.com

PHOTO CREDITS: page 20: ©Gene Martin Collection / Alamy Stock Photo

Quote source: Feliciano Enterprises. "Biography." José Feliciano: https://www.josefeliciano.com/biography

Edited by: Hailey Scragg
Illustrations by: Elisa Chavarri
Cover and interior layout by: J.J. Giddings

Library of Congress PCN Data

José Feliciano / Annette M. Clayton
(Leaders Like Us)
ISBN 978-1-73165-739-8 (hardcover)
ISBN 978-1-73165-726-8 (softcover)
ISBN 978-1-73165-752-7 (e-book)
ISBN 978-1-73165-765-7 (e-pub)
Library of Congress Control Number: 2023933215

Rourke Educational Media
Printed in the United States of America
01-1982311937